Embracing Cultural Diversity
in the Workplace and in
Nursing Practice

April Eagle, MSN, RN

Embracing Cultural Diversity in the Workplace & in
Nursing Practice

Cornerstone Publishing
A Division of Cornerstone Creativity Group LLC
Phone: +1(516) 547-4999
info@thecornerstonepublishers.com
www.thecornerstonepublishers.com

To order bulk copies of this book or to contact the author please
email: **aeagle200@yahoo.com**

CONTENTS

SECTION ONE

NURSING THEORIES

MY PERSONAL STORIES

Cultural Diversity if not understood and/or embraced can cause a lot of problems in the workplace, and in Nursing practice. Before I go on, I just want to share some stories about my personal experience with discrimination and prejudice that I have suffered in the workforce as a Healthcare worker, and Nurse within the USA in the last 26 years. My story is not any different from what many others are experiencing daily. There are many individuals who choose to pay deaf ears to what they hear and/or what they see, instead of speaking up and intervening to protect victims that are being discriminated against.

On one occasion while working in a well-known Hospital in the North East, we had a staff meeting with the administrative team one morning. When I got to the meeting room, I signed in with my first and last name only because I did not see where it indicated that my credential was required. One of the top administrators coordinating the attendance wrote down CNA behind my name without first confirming my job title. This incident happened in 2008. To say that I was appalled is to say the least. I handled the situation right away by having a discussion with this individual about why she assumed that I was a Certified Nursing Assistant (CNA) without first confirming my credentials with me. This person then apologized profusely as she turned all red in her face. This incident was so upsetting for me. Another incident that happened while working as a Charge Nurse on the unit in this same Hospital was that while seated at the nursing station, I was approached by a patient's family member who was a Caucasian male. He looked directly at me with my badge clearly visible to him, asked that I call him the Nurse. I told him I was the nurse and his face just fell. This incident did not upset me as much as the other perpetrated by a top administrative person who should know better never to assume anything.

My education more than my skills and experience in Nursing seems to surprise a lot of persons when they meet me for the first time in my nursing practice. Many begin to question me about my advanced degree like it is an impossible feat to accomplish. Rather than get upset about this, I am just shocked about many people's ignorance when it comes to interpersonal interactions. Getting a degree is a personal choice, and no one has the authority to determine who qualifies or who can get an education or pursue an advance degree. I have heard many times "I hear you have a Masters' degree," during casual office conversations from peers or supervisors.

Recently on a travel assignment to the West coast, I could feel the tension around me from some people that work in the Hospital. These are persons from top management to staff who work side by side me on the units. At first, some of them tried to intimidate me but that did not work, because I am not easily intimidated by anyone. I reported some incidents that occurred to the unit manager who did nothing to address them. Secondly, the unit manager had asked me from the beginning that "why would a Masters-prepared nurse be working as a travelling nurse?" My response was that it was a personal choice from a decision I made to get away from home for a while. During and towards the end of my contract, I asked twice to be extended for a few weeks through my agency because I saw the staffing need the facility had, but my requests were declined both times. Even when I requested to make up two weeks that I had taken off work due to a family emergency in order to complete my 13 weeks assignment, my request was still not granted. Three days after my contract ended, my recruiter contacted me and told me that the same facility was requesting that they send 3 nurses to work for them. I already told my recruiter that I believe they did not welcome me in that facility because of the vibes I felt, but my recruiter dismissed it and did not want to believe my concern.

So, she re-submitted my profile again the third time, and immediately it was refused. The reason they gave was that "it was a "personality issue." Mind you, the references given to me by two managers were excellent regarding my skills, clinical competence, work ethics, interpersonal interactions with others, etc. But there was something about me that they didn't like, I guess it was my confidence and knowledge in practice. I got along with almost everyone except a handful of persons that I worked with who did not want to be held accountable. As a professional nurse I try to maintain my professionalism with peers whether they like me or not. Can you imagine being discriminated against because of your personality? It was more than that. It was about my race, education, confidence in practice, and the ability not to allow myself to be bullied on the job. If I wasn't a strong person this sort of rejection in the workplace is enough to break somebody and cause them to fall into depression. I understand the game, so I do not allow other people's behaviors taint my heart and soul. I keep it moving because for every rejection & a No, there are many acceptances & Yeses. For me, this facility exhibited the "White Privilege" attitude that no matter how qualified and experienced one is in the profession, they decide who stays among them and who leaves. I left this facility to a better paying and more accepting work environment. I have learnt over the years what battles to fight, and the ones that I just leave alone. At the end of the day their decision is not a reflection of me, but of their discrimination against me because two other traveling Nurses were extended.

In another incident working for a renowned Hospital on the East Coast, one morning a Caucasian female colleague walked into the office and said "Hello Monkeys" to another African American peer and I. Mind you both of us were the only black employees working in that environment, and it was the two of us only that were in the office when she came in that morning. I was shocked that someone could be so ignorant as to call two black women monkeys. I turned to her and asked her why she would use such words as a greeting. She got red in the face and stammered as she said sorry and stated that she did not think it was offensive. I told her never to use such a word with me or another black person ever. She apologized profusely and walked out of the room. The other person was too timid to say anything, and she told me I should not have spoken up but report the incident to the supervisor. I educated her on the spot that I'd rather correct the colleague's ignorance instead of getting her into trouble.

The last experience I want to share involved another individual who decided he was going to micromanage me while he was assuming an interim supervisory position, while the Military officer assigned to the position was yet to arrive. He did so many petty things, his behavior became laughable for others to notice his bad behaviors towards me. Daily, he will enter my office multiple times without knocking, just to tell me he forgot what he came into my office for. By the end of 4 months of him being in that role, I developed depression, heartburn, and became anxious around him. I had to put in my resignation prematurely because of his behaviors.

Many employees experience distressing symptoms such as the ones described above due to bullying, intimidation, gossips, verbal abuse from superiors & peers, and discriminations of all sorts. In nursing practice, there is a popular saying that "the older nurses eat their young ones alive." The young nurses are not the only ones who experience some of these traumatic workplace discriminations, and negative behaviors from peers. There are many ignorant people in all spheres of work life. It could be in the school systems, politics, religious settings, marketplace, corporate & business world, healthcare, and nursing practice, etc.

As co-workers we must be careful about the jokes we make, and the things we say around other people who we do not know that well. A joke may be accepted by some peers who know you well and understand your personality from years of working with you. This may not be the case for someone just getting to know you.

Reflective Thinking

This section requires group discussion and participation

1. What are your thoughts regarding the experiences of the discriminations described above?

2. How would you have reacted to the individuals involved?

3. Can you share some of the discriminations you have experienced, and how did they make you feel?

4. Do you have some prejudices and biases against people of a different race than you?

5. If you noticed that someone is being discriminated against, would you intervene or say something to the perpetrator?

6. Have you ever been misunderstood by someone from a different race because of what you said?

7. If someone accuse you of been discriminatory, how would you respond?

April Eagle, MSN, RN

Reflective Responses

Reflective Responses

UNDERSTANDING THE NEED OF NURSING THEORIES IN PRACTICE

As a nurse, one must be able to practice using one or two Nursing Model-theories that identifies with the core of a Nurse's practice. These two Nursing theorists have influenced my nursing practice because of their philosophical beliefs about the nursing profession. Jean Watson's philosophy and science of caring has guided my practice as an empathetic and compassion nurse, while Madeleine Leininger's Transcultural Nursing theory has assisted me in having an open mind in my nursing practice as I care for people from all walks of life. And as I also interact with peers, superiors, and vendors on the job.

The four major concepts of Jean Watson's Philosophy and Science of Caring are: Human being, Health, Environment/society, and Nursing.

1. Human beings are to be valued, respected, nurtured, understood, and assisted during care encounters.

2. Health is being in a place of our highest level of overall physical, mental, social functioning in the absence

of illness, and/or the presence of efforts leading to wellness.

3. Environment: Watson's ideology is that Nurses have existed from generation to generation caring for others as a way of dealing with illness in societies where Nurses live in, which is unique to the nursing practice.

4. Nursing: This model states that Nursing is all about health promotion, illness prevention, healing the sick, and health restoration. The focus of nursing is promotion of health, wellness, and healing. Watson's belief is that patient-centered care or holistic care is central to nursing practice in patient care. Watson defines nursing as "a human science of persons and human health-illness experiences that are mediated by professional, personal, scientific, esthetic and ethical human transactions." (Nursing Theory, 2020).

Watson's model makes seven assumptions:

1. Caring can be demonstrated and practiced effectively only during interpersonal interactions.

2. Caring consists of nursing measures that result in the satisfaction of certain human needs.

3. Effective caring must promote health, the individual or family growth.

4. Caring responses accept patients from when they enter the care environment until the end of the care encounter.

5. A caring environment is supposed to provide holistic care which offers opportunity for the patient to choose

the best action for himself or herself at a given point in time during the care transaction.

6. A science of caring is as important as the science of curing because they complement one another.

7. The practice of caring is the bedrock of nursing.

Madeleine Leininger's Transcultural Nursing theory

The concepts of this Theory are as follows:

1. Cultures are used to understand people's behaviors

2. Acknowledges that there are diverse cultures

3. Cultures influences all area of an individual's life- it defines health and sickness, and how one seeks for treatment and resolution to sicknesses and distresses.

4. Every individual is unique and possess many differences that separates them from another human being. And their individuality must be respected

5. Cultural competence must be embraced and used in Nursing practice. Cultural competence is a combination of culturally congruent behaviors, practice attitudes, and policies that enable the Nurse care effectively in a multicultural workplace. (Sagar 2012)

Regardless of the work environment one is in, the knowledge and application of Watson and Leininger's theories in our daily interactions with others will help foster and maintain a conflict free workplace. When persons care, and respect people from different backgrounds from theirs the gains are endless. We must interact professionally in a Caring, Empathetic, and Compassionate way.

Reflective Thinking

1. Are you a caring person?

2. When interacting with others, do you consider their personal & cultural beliefs systems

3. Are you respectful of others regardless of their cultural background?

4. Do you interact with others in a caring, empathetic, and/or compassionate way?

5. What are your biases and prejudices?

6. Do you have an understanding of Emotional Intelligence?

7. Do you know yourself?

Reflective Responses

Reflective Responses

SECTION 2

CULTURAL DIVERSITY

CULTURAL DIVERSITY

What does it mean?

Cultural Diversity is defined as the "existence of multiplicity of sub-cultures and different value systems in a plural or multicultural society or other setting (Businessdictionary.com, 2013).

- Globalization, travel, & global health
- Nursing shortage
- Migration of foreign nurses to the West

The U.S. population is growing and becoming increasingly more diverse due to factors such as globalization, travel, global health, nursing shortage and migration of foreign nurses to the West.

Globalization: In a broad sense has been defined as a constellation of processes by which nations, businesses, and people are becoming more connected and interdependent via increased economic integration and communication exchange, cultural diffusion (especially of the Western culture) and travel (Falk-Rafael, 2006).

"Understanding the concept of globalization has significant implications not only for the world health and international politics, but also for the health of individuals......It is important that nurses appreciate that globalization does not pertain solely to realms of economy theory and world politics, but also that it impacts on our daily nursing practice and the welfare of our patients." (Davidson et al., 2003). The closer interactions of human activity as a result of globalization have great implications for the world as well as for the nursing profession.

Global health: Is a concept that integrates a burden of disease approach with social, political, and environmental contexts (Falk-Rafael, 2006).

According to the U.S Department of Health and Human Services report, "the U.S. will require 1.2 million new RNs by 2014 to meet the nursing needs of the country, 500, 000 to replace those leaving practice and an additional 700,000 new RNs to meet growing demands for nursing services." (Potera, 2009). "The RN workforce is expected to grow from 2.9 million in 2016 to 3.4 million in 2026, an increase of 438,100 or 15%. The Bureau also project the need for an additional 203,700 new RNs each year through 2026 to fill newly created positions and to replace retiring nurses." (aacn.org, 2020).

It was reported that "in this age of globalization, many countries have turned to overseas' recruitment to fill vacancies caused by a limited or unwilling locally trained workforce." Foreign-trained nurses accounted for 4% in the US in 2000."

In a 2008 report "An estimated 170,235 registered nurses (RN) living in the US received their initial nursing education in another country or a US territory, comprising 5.6% of the US nursing population, compared with 3.7% in 2007. About half of the internationally educated RNs living in the US in 2008 were from the Philippines, with another 11.5% from Canada, and 9.4% from India." (Strategiesfornursemanagers. com, 2013).

Of the approximately 90,000 foreign-educated nurses in the United States, California ranks (25, 717)first in state of employment followed by Florida (9,627), New York (9,337), Texas (6,738), New Jersey (6,160), Illinois (5,060), and others States (27,221). (nfap, 2007).

In other States, this may represent a small but important number, nonetheless.

Cultural Competence

5- Component Model for developing cultural competence in care encounters

- Cultural awareness
- Cultural knowledge
- Cultural skill
- Cultural encounter
- Cultural desire

The culturally competent nursing care requires the understanding and use of the 5-component model for developing cultural competence in care encounters. These are: Cultural awareness, cultural knowledge, cultural skill, cultural encounter, and cultural desires.

"Developing an awareness of one's own existence, sensations, thoughts, and environment without letting it have an undue influence on those from other backgrounds; demonstrating knowledge and understanding of the client's culture; accepting and respecting cultural differences; adapting care to be congruent with the client's culture." (Flowers, 2004).

Cultural awareness: Involves self-examination and in-depth exploration of one's own cultural and professional background. (Cultural awareness should begin with insight into one's own cultural health-care beliefs and values).

We as nurses must first understand our own cultural background and explore, identify, and recognize possible biases and prejudices towards other cultures. And if these exists, we must work to overcome them through cultural education.

Cultural knowledge: Involves the process of seeking and obtaining information based on different cultural and ethnic groups.

We must seek to engage with patients and their families in order to learn about their culture, and some cultural beliefs regarding healthcare practices.

Cultural skill: Involves the ability of the nurse to collect relevant cultural data regarding the client's presenting problem and accurately perform a culturally specific physical assessment. (A framework which supports this method of assessment includes such elements as communication, space, social organization, time, environmental control, and biological variations).

Being aware and able to skillfully maintain some reasonable distance during care encounters with patients whose cultural beliefs include avoidance of touch/physical closeness during interactions. Recognizing how each patient view & respond to pain based on cultural beliefs.

Cultural encounter: Is defined as the process that encourages nurses to directly engage in cross-cultural interactions with patients from culturally diverse backgrounds.

A nurse intentionally engaging in cross-cultural interactions during care encounters. Asking questions in order to gain some understanding of patient's cultural beliefs and practices.

Cultural desire: Refers to the motivation to become culturally aware and to seek cultural encounters. Inherent in cultural desire is the willingness to be open to others, to accept and respect cultural differences, and be willing to learn from others.

Being open and willing to learn at every opportunity that presents itself in the patient-care environment.

Labeling and generalizing those who are different, based on global and ignorant stereotypes are major contributors to the problem of being culturally uneducated.

Achieving cultural education is a team effort. Members of a particular culture and ethnic group must be willing to share information while practicing a great deal of patience. (Seibert et al., 2002).

The Culture Exercise

Use the images and flags to provide examples of some identified cultural characteristics for the group.

Culture is one of the most influential of all the factors known to play a vital role in health beliefs, values, and practices.

Reflective Responses

SECTION 3

CULTURAL COMPETENCE

CASE STUDIES

Case Study #1

An ER nurse in a small rural hospital witnessed the admission of an elderly Native American man, who was brought in by his wife, sons, and daughters. The patient had a history of 2 previous MIs, and his current clinical findings suggested he was having another one. During his initial assessment, he calmly informed the ER staff and doctor that, other than coming to the hospital, he was following the "old ways" of dying. He reported that he had "made peace with God and was ready to die" and "wanted his family with him." Regardless of the man's wishes, medical interventions were ordered and performed, and patient was transferred to an ICU of a regional hospital 3 hours away. He died 2 weeks later after 2 code blues, intubation, and receiving mechanical ventilation for most of the time. Only his wife was at his bedside, the other family members were unable to be there due to financial cost of traveling to the facility. This man's cultural values and preferences in relation to dying were disregarded (Flowers, 2004).

Ethic committee, Advanced directives and providing support to the patient and family were issues not addressed in this scenario.

"Lack of cultural awareness and failure to provide culturally competent care can greatly increase the stresses experienced by critically ill patients and can result in inadequate care provided by healthcare professionals" (Flowers, 2004).

Case Study #2

In a study of American-Chinese and Taiwanese patients' perceptions of dyspnea and related nursing actions during their admissions to ICU after cardiac surgery, Chinese patients reported their beliefs that physical energy was depleted during a dyspnea episode and that uninterrupted rest, sleep, and nutritional support allowed the body to recover afterwards. Lack of awareness of these concerns among the ICU nurses resulted in several comments offered by one Chinese patient which stated that he wrote down 'eating, wife,' he wanted his wife to prepare his favorite food for him. But the American nurse did not understand the patient's request/need, and she suggested that patient relax and sleep again. Pt reported "but, how can I relax? I needed the homemade food cooked with herbs, and only my wife knew how to make it. I did not request it again since I was afraid that they might think that I was odd and look down on me." Awareness of patient's cultural beliefs was not incorporated into his care.

THE BENEFITS OF CULTURAL COMPETENCE

- Improved nurse-patient interactions
- Understanding patients' behaviors
- Not making assumptions about
- Cultural beliefs about gender roles, and
- Better Patient/family education

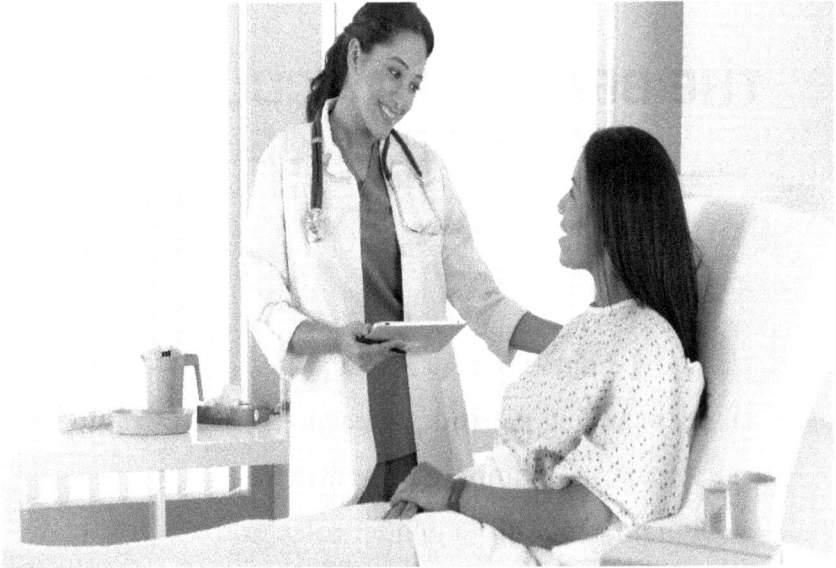

As much as we as professional Nurses want to be culturally sensitive and competent in the care of patients, there is also the need to practice cultural sensitivity and awareness in our various clinical settings in our interactions and relationship with co-workers, stakeholders, and vendors of the Healthcare organization one works for. This apply in other work environment as well. We must consider the dignity, respect, and feelings of other in interpersonal interactions and communications.

The benefits of a culturally sensitive and competent work environment are safety, support, trust, motivation, improved workflow, increased productivity, teamwork, and success.

- Increased Teamwork & Collaboration
- Reduced conflicts between co-workers
- Improved patient-care outcomes, and
- Improved interpersonal communication
- Success

Summary

Diversity in the workplace and in nursing practice will continue to bring those organizations that value it, increased productivity and conflict free work environments, improved patient-care delivery and better patient-care outcomes. We all bring to the workplace unique talents, cultural experiences, and ways of thinking that when mixed together the result is the creation of better ways of thinking and doing things. And more happy ad satisfied customers, employees, and employers.

Good luck as you conscientiously and consistently embrace cultural diversity in your organizations.

Reflective thinking

1. What are your thoughts after reading through this book?

2. How would you improve in your interpersonal and interprofessional relationships with others that are different than you?

3. Are there major areas of improvement that you will need to work on in order not to offend others?

4. If you witness someone that is being discriminated against, would you report it to a supervisor, or discuss it with the parties involved first?

Reflective Responses

REFERENCES

Batata, A.S. (2005). Research: International nurse recruitment and NHS vacancy: a cross-sectional analysis. Globalization and health, 1(7). doi: 10.1186/1744-8603-1-7

Businessdictionary.com (2013). Retrieved from: http://www.businessdictionary.com/definition/cultural-diversity.html

Davidson, P.M., Meleis, A., Daly, J., & Douglas, M.M. (2003). Globalization as we enter the 21st Century: Reflections and directions for nursing education, science, research and clinical practice. Contemporary Nurse, 15(3), 162-74. Retrieved from: http://www.ncbi.nlm.nih.gov/pubmed/14649522

Falk-Rafael, A. (2006). Globalization, and global health: Toward nursing praxis in the global community. Advances in nursing science, 29(1), 2-14. Retrieved from: http://journals.lww.com

Flowers, D.L. (2004). Culturally competent nursing care: A challenge for the 21 Century [e-letter]. Retrieved from: http://ccn.aacnjournals.org/content/24/4/48.full

https://image.slidesharecdn.com/pptpresentation-dr-131020170155-phpapp01/95/transcultural-nursing-powerpoint-presentationdr-madeleine-leininger-10-638.jpg?cb=1382288976 nfap (2007). Foreign-educated nurses : A small but important part of the U.S. Health workforce. National Foundation for American Policy. Retrieved from: http://www.nfap.com/pdf/071003nurses.pdf

Nursing Theory: Watson's Philosophy and Science Caring (2020). Retrieved from (https://nursing-theory.org/theories-and-models/watson-philosophy-and-science-of-caring.php)

Potera, C. (2009). The nursing shortage. AJN, American journal of nursing, 109(1), p22. doi: 10.1097/01.NAJ.0000344026.43038.9b

Seibert, P.S., Stridh-Igo, P., and Zimmerman. C.G. (2002). A checklist to facilitate cultural awareness and sensitivity. Journal of Medical Ethics, 28 (3), 143-146. doi: 10.1136/jme.28.3.143.

Strategiesfornursemanagers.com, (2013). Nursing workforce getting more diverse, older [e-letter]. Retrieved from: http://www.strategiesfornursemanagers.com/ce_detail/248744.cfm.

www.ingramcontent.com/pod-product-compliance
Lightning Source LLC
Chambersburg PA
CBHW070841300326
41935CB00038B/1318